Key

SOCIAL SAFETY NET LAWS

Cavendish
Square
New York

Alex Acks

Published in 2020 by Cavendish Square Publishing, LLC

243 5th Avenue, Suite 136, New York, NY 10016

Copyright © 2020 by Cavendish Square Publishing, LLC

First Edition

Website: cavendishsq.com

Cataloging-in-Publication Data

Names: Acks, Alex.
Title: Key social safety net laws / Alex Acks.
Description: New York : Cavendish Square Publishing, 2020. | Series: Laws that changed history | Includes glossary and index.
Identifiers: ISBN 9781502655325 (pbk.) | ISBN 9781502655332 (library bound) | ISBN 9781502655349 (ebook)
Subjects: LCSH: Public welfare--Law and legislation--United States--Juvenile literature. | Welfare recipients--Legal status, laws, etc.--United States--Juvenile literature. | Welfare recipients--Medical care--Government policy--United States--Juvenile literature.
Classification: LCC KF3720.A93 2020 | DDC 344.7303'16--dc23

Printed in China

CONTENTS

Introduction

At the end of 2018, President Donald Trump demanded $5.7 billion in funds to build a wall between the United States and Mexico—a project that was unpopular with most Americans at that time.[1] The Republican-controlled House of Representatives refused to vote on a government funding bill the Senate had passed because it did not include money for the wall; without funding, on December 22, 2018, the federal government ran out of money to run nine of its departments.

Immediately, more than 800,000 people employed by the federal government could not be paid. About 380,000 of them were furloughed: They were told to go home and not return to work until there was funding. The other 420,000 workers were forced to continue working with no idea of when their next paycheck would come.[2] The shutdown affected even more people indirectly. Government janitors lost pay because the buildings they normally cleaned were shut down. Federal workers no longer had spare income to spend at local businesses such as restaurants. Economic growth slowed in the United States as a whole.

As the shutdown continued, another threat arose. Programs that were important parts of the social safety net, such as food stamps, were in danger of running out of money if Congress and the president couldn't reach an agreement.[3] As workers missed paychecks, many filed for unemployment insurance[4] and lined up at food banks.[5] Some state and local governments intervened directly to provide emergency aid to keep workers from being evicted from their homes and to shore up food programs.[6]

After thirty-five days, President Trump agreed to sign a short-term bill with no funding for his wall so employees could come back to work and the government could resume services. This was the longest shutdown of the federal government in United States history as of 2019.

The shutdown revealed strengths of the social safety net in the United States, as 800,000 people suddenly had to be caught from financial free-fall. It also revealed terrifying weaknesses, such as just how many people with what are considered good-paying jobs are only one or two paychecks away from disaster. Programs almost ran out of money and had to be shored up by the states, and the assumption that federal employment is secure was proven to be false.

A 2017 CareerBuilder report showed that 78 percent of Americans live paycheck-to-paycheck, meaning they don't have much in savings and a missed paycheck could mean financial ruin.[7] According to the Government Accountability Office, 20 percent of families in which someone earns only the federal minimum wage lived in poverty in 2016—and consistently used social safety net programs.[8]

The social safety net as we know it in the United States is less than 100 years old and has been marked for reform and destruction almost since its beginning. The fate of the social safety net in America can perhaps be found in the answer to a larger question we've asked ourselves since the founding of the nation: What is our duty to our fellow citizens, particularly those less fortunate than ourselves?

Without a Net

The social safety net as we understand it in modern America is a set of programs intended to help the needy, hopefully in a way that will lift them out of poverty long-term. Charities or other institutions often run such programs; the largest programs are run by the federal government and are available to the entire country. The idea that the federal government should have a part in the social safety net is relatively recent, however.

Workhouses and Poorhouses

Before the founding of the United States, the main source of aid for the poor—people who were often elderly, disabled, orphaned, or widowed—was determined locally. "Overseers of the poor," who were generally middle class or wealthy men, would sort poor people who needed help into two categories: deserving or undeserving. The "deserving" poor

Charles Dickens used poorhouses and workhouses in his fiction, but they were real. People were forced to work and live in miserable conditions.

were thought to be blameless according to the morals of the day and might be given monetary aid. The "undeserving" poor faced harsher choices, including being sent to the poorhouse.

Poorhouses and workhouses are concepts familiar from the novels of Charles Dickens—dark, grim places where children were forced to work in dirty conditions and were barely fed. When English people came to America, they established workhouses there as well, along with other practices that targeted poor people, such as banishment or being auctioned off as indentured servants.

By the 1800s, the poorhouse was the model that dominated in America. Conditions in poorhouses were unhealthy and terrible, often on purpose as a way to punish people for being poor. Over time, the population of poorhouses and workhouses shifted so there was a large, permanent number of inmates who were elderly, disabled, or "immoral" women. More able-bodied male workers moved in and out of the poorhouses as they found work. Anne Sullivan, the woman who eventually became activist Helen Keller's teacher, grew up in a poorhouse. She described it as "a crime against childhood."

Poorhouses remained the main method of local governments for dealing with the undeserving poor up until the Great Depression.[1]

Mutual Aid Societies

Without public welfare programs, health insurance, or labor protections, those in the working class were never far from the poorhouse. What little money they made allowed them to band together into mutual aid societies, fraternal benefit societies, and unions.

These societies could be small local groups or massive, country-spanning organizations. For example, by 1919, the Modern Woodmen of America had more than 1 million members.

The Modern Woodmen of America was one kind of fraternal organization, providing mutual aid to other members of the organization.

They were often organized around a common identity, such as profession, religion, or race. Members generally paid fees to join the society, then participated in fundraising activities that provided more money to run the group. In return, mutual aid societies helped provide health care (large ones even ran their own hospitals), banking, and unemployment aid. They also promised to take care of widows and orphans if the main breadwinner of the household died.

Some of these societies still exist in modern America, such as the Knights of Columbus, though they have become less necessary—and therefore less popular—with the advent of employer-provided health insurance and other social safety net programs.[2]

The Locust Plagues of 1873–1877

Even massive natural disasters did little to encourage government interest in providing a safety net. Farmers had begun to spread rapidly west after the American Civil War, taking advantage of what was effectively a massive government giveaway of land that had been taken from Native Americans.

At the start of the 1870s, a drought plagued the American West and Midwest, threatening the livelihoods of many farmers. Worse, the drought created conditions perfect to cause the now-extinct Rocky Mountain locust to swarm and descend on farms, destroying whole crops. In 1875, one swarm of locusts was estimated to have covered more land area than the entire state of California and consisted of 12.5 trillion insects. The locusts ranged north from Saskatchewan and south to Texas, west from Colorado and east to Minnesota. Everywhere they went, they left starvation and poverty in their wake.

Some counties attempted to help the impoverished farmers by paying bounties for dead locusts or providing small amounts of direct aid, but the largely rural counties had little money to

In the 1800s, natural disasters such as locust plagues didn't spur the government to help its citizens any more quickly; politicians accused farmers of not really needing the help.

Coxey's Army

In 1893, the collapse of two major businesses set off a four-year economic depression. Unemployment rose to more than 10 percent. Jacob Coxey, an Ohio businessman, proposed that the federal government put the jobless to work building roads and improving infrastructure—an idea forty years ahead of its time. He launched a plan to pressure the government with a march on Washington, DC.

Armies of unemployed men and women from across the country joined Coxey. When Coxey's group reached its destination, it was as many as 10,000 strong. Coxey attempted to read his "Good Roads Bill" on the Capitol steps and was stopped by police wielding clubs, who beat the protestors back. Coxey spent twenty days in a workhouse for the crime of walking on the Capitol lawn.[3]

begin with—and some county governments were suspicious of the farmers, all but accusing them of not really requiring help.

State governments were even less helpful than county governments, with Minnesota the prime example. The Minnesota legislature set aside $20,000 in aid and extended property tax deadlines, but it also required farmers to sell all their livestock before they could be given relief, which might be as little as $4 per year; a family of four needed at least $200 to survive. Farmers were advised to consider eating locusts. The federal government eventually sent $100,000 in aid, while eastern newspapers complained, "It is humiliating to have [the farmers] so constantly before us, passing round the hat."[4]

The deep suspicion of anyone requiring help and the attitude that all problems were somehow the fault of those facing them, even problems such as a plague of locusts, showed that the idea of deserving and undeserving poor was still going strong—and revealed the ugly truth that all those in poverty were thought to be undeserving.

Workers' Compensation Laws

Since the fate of entire families rested on the ability of the men, women, and even children to work and earn wages, a single industrial accident or bad illness could doom anyone to the poorhouse. With the growth of unions in the Gilded Age, workers' insurance and workers' compensation became the first frontier of a true safety net.

The idea of workers' compensation was old even at that time. A tablet from 2050 BC Sumeria detailed monetary compensation for various on-the-job injuries workers could sustain. Other cultures developed their own types of compensation for lost body parts and injuries.

Modern workers' compensation got its start in Prussia under Chancellor Otto von Bismarck. Although he banned the Marxist and socialist parties that politically annoyed him, he picked up their most popular causes, such as social insurance. In 1884, he saw to the passage of workers' accident insurance. Later, he created public pension insurance that provided compensation for workers who fell ill or had injuries unrelated to their jobs.

The United States paid close attention to these developments, as journalists and authors such as Upton Sinclair pushed awareness of the hideous working conditions in factories into the public eye. States attempted to pass their own workers' compensation laws as early as 1898, though these laws were largely unsuccessful or too limited.

Wisconsin passed the first comprehensive law in 1911; the other states followed, with Mississippi coming in last in 1948. The first thread of a social safety net had been put in place.[5]

13

The Great Depression

The 1920s brought an economic boom to the United States, with factories cranking out new, exciting technologies such as cars and radios. Silent movies gave workers a new kind of entertainment to spend their money on. While business boomed, with company profits increasing as much as 65 percent, wages for workers increased only 8 percent. The wealth gap was such that the top 0.1 percent of Americans had as much income as the 42 percent at the bottom combined. The shiny new toys of the 1920s were bought largely on credit, and those who had money speculated on the stock market, accepting risk for the promise of big money on the other side.

The Roaring Twenties crashed to a halt with the collapse of the stock market on October 29, 1929, which came to be known as Black Tuesday. An economic crash and depression, far worse than the one that had occurred in 1893, spread across the world. By 1932, 25 percent of the American workforce—about 15 million people—was unemployed as banks failed and took businesses with them.[1]

In 1929, the stock market collapsed. The economic crash that followed left millions of people poor and unemployed.

Without a safety net to catch them, millions of people lost the homes they owned or rented. Some were lucky enough to have family they could squeeze in with in increasingly overcrowded apartments. Hundreds of thousands ended up on the streets. They created large encampments and shantytowns that squatted on empty public land. One of the largest such encampments in the United States was in Seattle. It covered 9 acres (3.6 hectares) of land, had a population of around 1,200, and had its own community government, including a mayor.[2]

These homeless encampments became known as "Hoovervilles," pointing the finger at the person many of those suffering held responsible: President Herbert Hoover. Hoover focused on trickle-down relief ideas, believing that if the government uplifted businesses, the positive effect would "trickle down" to workers.

RFC, FERA, and the WPA

As the Great Depression deepened, President Hoover remained reluctant to provide direct relief to those suffering, even blocking legislation, but he did pass the Reconstruction Finance Corporation Act in January 1932. This law created the Reconstruction Finance Corporation (RFC), which gave loans to businesses to help them stay afloat. An amendment in July 1932, which renamed the law the Emergency Relief and Construction Act, expanded the RFC's power. It could now set aside funds for public works projects, such as an expansion to the Brooklyn Navy Yard, and give states money for relief efforts. However, Hoover's slow response to the financial crisis led to him receiving only 39.7 percent of the popular vote in the next election, a humiliating defeat at the hands of Democratic challenger Franklin D. Roosevelt. The new president promised immediate action to combat the Depression, with a sweeping round of proposals known as the New Deal.

President Roosevelt signed the Federal Emergency Relief Act on May 2, 1933, expanding greatly on what Hoover had started by creating the Federal Emergency Relief Administration (FERA). Rather than giving out loans, FERA offered grants to states for public works projects and paid direct relief to individuals.

In 1933, Roosevelt signed an executive order to create the Civil Works Administration (CWA). This organization, which received part of its funding from FERA, set out a series of public works projects that gave unskilled laborers temporary employment through that winter. CWA put men to work building roads and schools and gave women jobs such as sewing clothing that was distributed to the poor.

Congress disbanded the CWA on March 31, 1934. A little over a year later, the Emergency Relief Appropriation Act gave Roosevelt funding to create the Works Progress Administration (WPA), which oversaw more public works projects and permanently shifted the relief model to offering jobs. The WPA

The Civilian Conservation Corps

Franklin Roosevelt was personally interested in conservation and nature and had a vision of how this interest could provide work for young, unemployed men. He created the Civilian Conservation Corps (CCC) with an executive order on April 5, 1933. Over the next 9 years, almost 3 million men (88,000 of them Native American) worked under the guidance of the National Park Service. The US Army was called on to perform a massive peacetime mobilization to transport CCC employees to work camps in the West.

took over FERA's duties and expanded on them until 1943, when World War II ended the Great Depression.

Not only did the WPA oversee the modern equivalent of $194 billion worth of infrastructure and building construction projects, it employed artists in Federal Project Number One, which included a historical records survey and federally funded music and theater performances and art exhibitions.[3]

The Social Security Act

Out-of-work Americans demanded a system of social insurance that could protect the sick, disabled, and elderly. Roosevelt agreed with the idea; on January 17, 1935, he asked Congress to create social security legislation. Seven months later, on August 14, he had it on his desk.

The Social Security Act (SSA) created old-age pensions that were funded by taxes on the payrolls of businesses and the wages of the self-employed. It also provided funds to help children, the blind, and the unemployed. It established Aid to Families with Dependent Children (AFDC), a grant program to provide welfare payments that would help children who had lost a parent or weren't being fully supported. AFDC allowed states to determine what "need" meant and set their own benefit levels, though with federally determined requirements.

The unemployment insurance programs the SSA prompted were run by the states and funded with grants from the federal government. These provided payments to people who had become unemployed, to help bridge the gap between losing one job and finding the next.[4]

Federal Houses for the Homeless

As part of the New Deal, the Public Works Administration (PWA) was directed to give loans and grants to state and local governments for public works projects, such as bridges, dams,

Posters such as this one were displayed in post offices during the New Deal to instruct people on how to apply for the new social security program.

From 1934 to 1937, the PWA built housing projects across the United States, including the one shown here in New York City's Harlem neighborhood.

airports, sewers, and roads. The grants and loans allowed states to create construction jobs for the unemployed. The PWA was also directed to build low-income housing, but as this was not the organization's priority, it built relatively few—only 25,000 across the country, which wasn't enough to meet demand. The Housing Act of 1937 replaced the PWA Housing Division with the US Housing Authority and sped up the construction of low-income housing.

In 1934, another bill—the National Housing Act—created the Federal Housing Administration (FHA) to insure mortgages so more people would be able to buy houses. This encouraged private developers to build more homes and ultimately led to an increase in home ownership from 40 percent when the FHA was created to 68.1 percent in 2001.[5]

For all the good intentions of relieving the housing shortage, the execution of these programs was often racist. Housing projects built by the PWA were initially meant for white families; eventual projects for black families were segregated.[6] The FHA often refused to insure mortgages near black neighborhoods, a practice called redlining that continues today.[7] The FHA subsidized suburban housing divisions earmarked for white homeowners and justified redlining by claiming that black homeowners would cause property values to go down.[8]

A social safety net, though still thin at times, now existed in America. However, it was not equal in its administration or in whom it aimed to catch up out of poverty.

The Great Society

When John F. Kennedy was nominated by the Democratic Party for president in 1960, he said in his acceptance speech, "The New Frontier is here whether we seek it or not. Beyond that frontier are uncharted areas of science and space, unsolved problems of peace and war, unanswered questions of poverty and surplus."[1]

After his election, he set forth an ambitious plan to bring the New Frontier into reality. Congress cooperated with President Kennedy to raise the minimum wage and Social Security benefits, create the volunteer Peace Corps, and pass a housing bill aimed at helping senior citizens and farmers.[2] Meanwhile, Congress proved more reluctant to pass some of Kennedy's bigger ideas, such as a civil rights bill, health-care reform, and more ambitious housing programs, such as the creation of the Department of Housing and Urban Affairs (also known as the Department of Housing and Urban Development, or HUD).

Kennedy's assassination on November 22, 1963, could have put an end to the plans he'd made to strengthen the safety net in America further. However, Lyndon B. Johnson, finding

President John F. Kennedy spoke of a "new frontier" in 1960. This involved plans to raise the minimum wage, provide Social Security benefits, create the volunteer Peace Corps, and pass a housing bill aimed at helping senior citizens.

himself unexpectedly president in the wake of the tragedy, took up Kennedy's unfinished business and folded it into his own vision: the Great Society.[3]

The "War on Poverty"

President Johnson, in his first State of the Union address in 1964, declared, "This administration today, here and now, declares unconditional war on poverty in America." More than 37 million people in America were living in poverty at that time.[4]

Many of the programs he pursued were similar to what had worked during the Great Depression. The Economic Opportunity Act of 1964 created the Office of Economic Opportunity, which focused on education, job skills, and employment as a path out of poverty. The Job Corps directly created 100,000 jobs for the poor, half of which were in conservation projects. At Johnson's direction, state and local governments created work-training programs to work in parallel with the national work-study program. Grants were aimed at the unemployed and loans at companies that would hire them.

Johnson also realized that employment alone wasn't the solution to helping the poor. His determination to build a Great Society that would bring "an end to poverty and racial injustice"[5] spread to other aspects of the safety net.

The Food Stamp Act of 1964

Under President Kennedy, there'd been a pilot program for food stamps, overseen by the Department of Agriculture and authorized by executive order. These food stamps were modeled after a program that ran from 1939 to 1943, which had allowed people to purchase one-dollar orange food stamps and then receive an additional free fifty-cent blue food stamp, up to their monthly food budget. The orange stamps could be spent on any kind of food (but not alcohol), while the blue stamps could only be used for government-designated surplus staple foods, or crops that produced more food than was needed.

Stores often advertised food stamp programs, letting shoppers know what kind of stamps their store could accept.

Kennedy's food stamp program got rid of the blue and orange stamps—and the designated surplus food. Instead, there was one kind of coupon that people purchased with a discount based on their monthly food budget to help them afford a healthy diet for their family size. These coupons could only be spent on nonimported food—with the exceptions of coffee, tea, and bananas—and not on alcohol or tobacco.

Under President Johnson, the Food Stamp Act of 1964 made the pilot programs permanent and national, though eligibility was left up to the states. One year later, there were already half a million people using the food stamp program.[6]

Caution: Cigarette Smoking May Be Hazardous to Your Health

In modern America, warning labels and safety information are incredibly common, but prior to the Great Society, these safety standards were not nationally required. Johnson signed the Fair Packaging and Labeling Act of 1966, which he said would "mean that the American family will get full and fair value for every penny, dime and dollar that the family spends." He also enhanced food safety laws and put truth-in-lending laws in place to protect borrowers from predatory lending practices.

The Cigarette Labeling and Advertising Act became the first major push against the deadly health effects of tobacco, requiring now-familiar caution labels on every pack of cigarettes. In 1972, President Richard Nixon followed Johnson's lead by creating the Consumer Products Safety Commission to ensure that products were safe and appropriately labeled, from bottles for medicines to children's toys. [7]

Education as Part of the Great Society

President Johnson viewed education as the best way to lift people from poverty and guarantee a better life for children. However, schools in poorer areas of the United States were suffering from a lack of funding, so Johnson passed the Elementary and Secondary Education Act of 1965.

Title I of the act gave funding directly to schools with students from predominately low-income families, which made up most of the money spent by the act. The hope was that increased funding would help close educational gaps between poor children in urban and rural schools and their middle-class, suburban peers.

Title II of the act funded preschool programs and gave schools money to fund libraries and textbook purchases because textbooks in poor schools tended to be out of date and in bad condition. Title III gave support for educational programming outside of normal school hours and helped isolated rural schools start special education programs.[8]

The research that helped prompt the act also indicated that a key to breaking the cycle of poverty was reaching out to young children in disadvantaged communities. Sargent Shriver, who designed the Peace Corps program for President Kennedy, teamed up with child development experts to create the Head Start program under the Office of Economic Opportunity. Aimed at children between the ages of three and five, it started as an eight-week summer camp. The program later expanded to have full-day and year-round services linked to communities through volunteers and local donations.

Later in 1965, Johnson signed the Higher Education Act (HEA), which persists today. This increased federal money going to universities and created a system of low-interest loans that students could take from the government. The HEA also created the National Teachers Corps, which helped train teachers specifically to go to low-income schools.

In 1966, Johnson signed the Child Nutrition Act. This act expanded the National School Lunch Program, which had been created in 1946 by President Harry Truman under the National School Lunch Act to help feed poor students. The 1966 act also created a school breakfast program. However, this program was so inadequate that the Black Panthers—a militant political group focused on improving the lives of black Americans— created a community Free Breakfast for Children program to fill in Johnson's program's gaps.[9]

Medicare and Medicaid

By the 1960s, most working adults got their health insurance through their employers, which is the model we still have today. People who could not work or were no longer working, particularly the elderly, found paying for health insurance unaffordable. In the early 1960s, only half of the elderly had any kind of health insurance, and the policies they could afford had inadequate coverage. Private insurance companies also looked for excuses to terminate the policies of the elderly because they were considered high-risk. This wasn't a problem only for the poor—even elderly people who had extensive savings in their retirement risked losing everything if they had a serious illness.

Discussions had begun in Congress about the issue and a social insurance solution in 1957, long before Johnson was president. It took eight years of hearings and debate in Congress for them to arrive at Medicare, a program of government-provided health insurance plans that covered hospital care and services from doctors outside of hospitals. Medicare wasn't its own law; it was added under Title XVIII of the SSA.

President Lyndon B. Johnson (*left*) signs the Medicare bill into law, with Vice President Hubert Humphrey (*center*) and former president Harry Truman (*right*) at his side.

It took eleven months after the passage of Medicare for the program to start. People aged sixty-five and older were covered with health insurance.[10] Medicare had another profound social effect—if hospitals wanted to receive Medicare payments, they had to comply with the Civil Rights Act. Across the United States, hospitals were forced to desegregate their waiting rooms and floors in less than four months.[11]

Alongside Medicare, another program was created under Title XIX of the SSA: Medicaid. Medicaid aimed to help those in poverty attain health care. Rather than providing federally guaranteed health insurance like Medicare, Medicaid was a joint program between the federal government and the states. The federal government set out minimum expectations for state health care programs, and in exchange it paid half of the costs.

While much of Johnson's Great Society endures today in some form, Medicare and Medicaid in particular laid the groundwork for an expanded social safety net.

Reforms Begin

When Johnson left office at the beginning of 1969, 24 million Americans were classified as living in poverty—13 million fewer than when he'd become president. He had advanced his goals to end segregation and help black families; when he left office, 27 percent of black people lived in poverty, compared to 55 percent in 1960.[1]

The backlash against the Great Society was immediate, partially driven by Johnson's efforts to bring about racial equality. In 1968, with the country rocked by the assassination of Dr. Martin Luther King Jr. and the riots that followed, Richard Nixon played on white resentments and campaigned in part on eliminating antipoverty programs that he called "wasteful."

After his election, President Nixon successfully killed the Office of Economic Opportunity. His Urban Affairs counselor, Daniel Moynihan, stated in a memo, "The time may have come when the issue of race could benefit from a period of 'benign neglect.'"[2] Certain civil rights measures, such as voting rights, had been popular outside of the South because they arguably

When Lyndon Johnson left office, Richard Nixon took swift action to eliminate social programs he felt were "wasteful," which included closing the Office of Economic Opportunity.

didn't challenge the privileges or systems that supported the white majority. Combined with American political traditions that regarded any intervention of the government in private industry with deep suspicion, social safety net programs that helped black families in poverty became easy targets for attack.[3]

The decade after the Great Society wasn't entirely devoted to its destruction, however. Richard Nixon, Gerald Ford, and Jimmy Carter expanded certain parts of the safety net to compensate for problems that they saw as pressing during their presidencies.

Supplemental Security Income

When Social Security was created in 1935, it set aside funding to help blind people. In 1950, it was expanded to cover adults with more disabilities. Some payments were intended to supplement or replace the incomes of poor people who were elderly or had disabilities. Administration and distribution of these payments to those in need was left to the states, which meant payment and eligibility requirements could vary wildly.

Supplemental Security Income (SSI) was created with Title XVI of the SSA, signed by President Nixon on October 30, 1972. Title XVI allowed the federal government to take over administration of these welfare payments and standardize eligibility so that it no longer seemed random or unfair. The program was set up to be means tested, meaning it would help only those with income and assets under a certain level.[4]

Women, Infants, and Children

Research throughout the 1960s pointed to malnutrition and hunger among children as a major issue, culminating with the 1969 final report from the White House Conference on Food, Nutrition, and Health stating that "there can be no doubt that hunger and malnutrition exist in America, and that some millions may be affected."

In 1972, Women, Infants, and Children (WIC) was added to the Child Nutrition Act of 1966 and set out on a two-year pilot program to supplement food for children and pregnant women. Pregnant women were targeted specifically because poor nutrition during pregnancy is associated with low birth weight and other health problems for infants. WIC was administered by the states and distributed payments used for foods placed on an approved list that prioritized nutritional

WIC is a program specifically for women, infants, and children, helping pregnant and post-partum low-income mothers feed their children.

Meals on Wheels

Some people have trouble getting sufficient nutrition because they are unable to leave the home due to age or disability. In 1972, the Older Americans Act was amended to allow for the delivery of prepared, nutritious food. There are many charities that deliver food to people at their homes, but the best-known and only federally funded one is Meals on Wheels.

Funding for Meals on Wheels is limited, so deliveries are generally made by volunteers rather than paid employees. The meals cover one-third of the daily recommended nutrition, though most meals normally cover 40–50 percent. The federal government covers about 30 percent of the cost of the meals, with the rest supplied by public and private partnerships. Currently, about 135 million meals are being delivered to needy people each year.[5]

value. Whole-wheat bread, fruits and vegetables, cheese, eggs, and baby formula are a few examples. In 1975, the program became permanent.[6]

Pell Grants and Federal Direct Student Loans

In 1972, Congress made changes to the Higher Education Act, tweaking the loans and grants from the HEA and allowing for-profit schools access to federal funds. Six years later, President Jimmy Carter signed the Middle Income Assistance Act, which provided more grants to low-income students and broadened who was eligible for grants. Undergraduate students from low-income families could receive Pell Grants to assist them with paying for tuition and fees. Unlike loans, these grants do not have to be paid back except in certain circumstances—for example, if the student drops out of school before completing their degree program.[7]

Section 8 Housing

In 1974, Congress amended the Housing Act of 1937, making it the Housing and Community Development Act. This new law created what became known as the Section 8 Program, which allowed the federal government to assist tenants with their rent; the renter paid 30 percent and the government the rest. This kind of assistance could be for units in a specific building

Lyndon B. Johnson (*right*) created the Department of Housing and Urban Development (HUD) to develop policies on housing throughout the country.

or for private housing chosen by individual tenants. Private housing can refuse to rent to Section 8 tenants in some states.

Landlords who receive Section 8 money aren't allowed to charge their tenants more than what the government calculates is the fair market rent for a unit and must allow government inspections to make sure they meet the standards set out by the Department of Housing and Urban Development (HUD). Payments for Section 8 housing are administered by local Public Housing Authorities (PHAs), and the number of units they can subsidize is determined by the funding Congress gives them each year.[8]

While the rents paid for Section 8 housing are supposed to cover upkeep, chronically underfunded PHAs can't provide for building maintenance, so public housing has become increasingly decrepit. As early as the 1990s, issues with HUD inspections of public housing surfaced: HUD claimed landlords hide major problems with quick fixes, while tenants claimed HUD lets dangerous units pass inspections. Additionally, as the FHA's de facto mission to maintain segregated housing faded away in the 1950s and 1960s, public housing that had been restricted to white families who were "barely poor" allowed poor black families to move in. As of 2015, about 44 percent of residents in public housing were black, and "Section 8" and "public housing" had become racist insults used against people in need of housing assistance.[9]

The Earned Income Tax Credit

By 1973, 3.1 million families were receiving AFDC welfare, compared to 1 million in 1964. This sparked major debate over the need to reform the welfare program and how best to financially help poor families.

In 1971, President Nixon proposed a Family Assistance Plan that would have a minimum income guarantee for working poor families. The chairman of the Senate Finance Committee, Russell Long, opposed the idea because it would give the most benefit to people who didn't earn anything, and he believed that would discourage people from working. Instead, Long wanted to supplement the wages of workers. This idea became the earned income tax credit (EITC) in 1975. Originally, the credit was for 10 percent of the first $4,000 a low-income person with children earned, which meant they could get a maximum of $400 back from the government.

The EITC was meant to be temporary—something to help the working poor and give them more money to spend in an economy that was going into recession. In 1978, the EITC was made permanent. It then increased over the years. In the 1990s, people without children were allowed to take the credit as well.[10]

While Nixon's Family Assistance Plan was ultimately replaced by the EITC, it showed an increasing awareness that there were people who worked who still required assistance and also an increasing desire to link the social safety net to work.

The "Welfare Queen"

In 1976, Ronald Reagan spoke to a crowd at a campaign rally about the social safety net. "In Chicago, they found a woman who holds the record," he said. "She used 80 names, 30 addresses, 15 telephone numbers to collect food stamps, Social Security, veteran's benefits for four nonexistent deceased veteran husbands, as well as welfare. Her tax-free cash income alone has been running $150,000 a year." As Reagan ran (unsuccessfully that year) for the Republican nomination for president, he frequently used the example of this "welfare queen," who was using a broken social safety net to cheat honest taxpayers of hundreds of thousands of dollars, heavily implying that she was just one among thousands—and that she was black.

There was, in fact, a woman in Chicago who had defrauded the federal government of about $8,000 by using four aliases. She also stole from private citizens. Her name was Linda Taylor, though she'd been born Martha Miller and registered on the 1930 census as white. Reagan's fictionalized story was used to imply that welfare fraud was widespread and uncontrolled. In reality, most people used the system honestly and genuinely needed the money. Furthermore, cheating on welfare was the very least of Taylor's crimes—which included kidnapping.

Linda Taylor set off a moral panic in Illinois, where by 1978, 84 percent of people thought that welfare and Medicaid fraud should be the highest legislative priority. The Illinois Department of Public Aid set up a fraud hotline, which received 10,047 calls in 1977. Cases of welfare overpayments, often due to administrative errors, had previously been administrative matters; now Illinois and other states began to criminalize them. A Department of Justice study from 1983 estimated annual AFDC overpayments to be between $376 million and

President Ronald Reagan helped contribute to the stereotype of the "welfare queen," or someone who didn't work for their benefits and existed only to defraud hardworking Americans.

$3.2 billion, an enormous range that illustrated just how ill-defined the problem really was. In contrast to the public image of people getting rich on welfare, the average standard of living for families receiving AFDC was low compared to the average family.

Ronald Reagan won the 1980 election mainly by spreading rumors of welfare queens and then promising to fix the problem—which didn't exist to the extent he claimed it did. Throughout his presidency, he continued to add to the tall tale he had built from Linda Taylor. By 1981, he was claiming that, "in addition to collecting welfare under 123 different names, she also had 55 Social Security cards."[1]

The concept of the welfare queen provided a handy excuse to attack parts of the social safety net, a new name for the moral righteousness of refusing to help the undeserving poor live in dignity.

The Family Support Act of 1988

Toward the end of Reagan's presidency, after two years of legislative negotiating, the Family Support Act was passed by Congress and signed into law. The act modified the way child support payments were handled and required states to start withholding income from people who hadn't been making those payments.

The act required that all states create a training program called Job Opportunities and Basic Skills (JOBS). These programs were supposed to provide adults on AFDC with training, education, and ultimately employment. States could design their own programs, but their programs had to be approved by the Secretary of Health and Human Services every two years. People on AFDC were required to participate in their state JOBS unless they were ill, incapacitated, elderly, already working, or serving as a full-time caregiver in the home.[2]

This was ultimately a reimagining of AFDC welfare, intended to make it

temporary assistance rather than permanent. Job training and education became the path to getting families off AFDC, with the goal of making families self-sufficient.

Despite numerous programs, government assistance often falls short. Many communities have stepped up to feed the hungry and shelter the homeless.

Budget Cuts

The greatest effect on the social safety net in the 1980s was not a single piece of legislation but rather the budgets that President Reagan signed into law. In 1982, the largest tax cuts in history were passed, reducing personal and corporate tax revenue for the government by $37.7 billion. The budget for that year also cut $35 billion in spending—$25 billion of which came from social safety net programs. In the following years, President Reagan didn't get cuts as large as he wanted, but Congress continued to cut the budgets of welfare programs.

These budget cuts hit the working poor the hardest; AFDC payments to working parents were almost entirely eliminated, and those who remained on the program had their benefits greatly reduced. The cuts also eliminated the Public Service Employment program, which had offered the unemployed jobs

In 1982, Ronald Reagan cut $25 billion from social safety net programs to deliver a tighter budget. Almost 1 million people were removed from the food stamp program alone.

The "Welfare Trap"

"Welfare trap" is a term for the concept that people receiving welfare do not have an incentive or ability to get off welfare. The term can be used in a descriptive or pejorative way, implying either that someone is trapped in a system with no way out or that they are lazy and want free money. Means testing for welfare may require people on welfare to have little or no savings, so if they get off welfare they can be knocked immediately into financial jeopardy. Taxes increase as people start working and are phased off welfare, meaning the wages they earn are worth far less than welfare benefits—so if they get a promotion, they actually make less money. This is called an income cliff.[3]

in nonprofits and state and local governments so they could gain experience and move into the private sector.

In 1982, the food stamp program cost $11.3 billion and served 22 million people. Congress placed a test on gross household income to limit the number of people who could participate, and it also decreased the frequency of cost-of-living adjustments, effectively meaning food stamps would lag in value behind the actual cost of groceries. This removed almost 1 million people from the food stamp program.[4]

The effect on the working poor was to reduce their living standards. Many working families who had been on AFDC before the budget cuts found themselves with less income than a nonworking family on AFDC because of taxes. Against predictions, the working poor families did not tend to quit their jobs to get back on AFDC; instead, they struggled through their reduced circumstances.[5]

The End of Welfare as We Know It

President Bill Clinton was elected at the tail end of a recession—one that had put 33 percent more families on AFDC. Due partially to years of talk of welfare queens, 81 percent of people responding to a *TIME*/CNN poll wanted reform of the welfare system, and even more believed that the welfare system of the time stopped poor people from looking for work. Between his election and his reelection, Clinton vetoed two strict welfare reform bills authored by the Republican-controlled Congress; when they presented him with one in 1996 that was significantly less harsh, he signed it on August 22. He coasted to reelection having then fulfilled a campaign promise he made in 1991: He would "end welfare as we have come to know it."[1]

The Personal Responsibility and Work Opportunity Reconciliation Act of 1996

"Personal responsibility" related to welfare was a phrase introduced by Ronald Reagan, in parallel with his tales of welfare queens. He used the idea of responsibility to mean a mechanism of accountability: The idea was that if someone was poor because

In 1996, President Bill Clinton signed welfare reform into law, having promised in 1991 that he meant to change the way people thought of welfare.

they had made bad decisions, they did not deserve help from the government.[2] This is another incarnation of the deserving versus the undeserving poor. The idea of personal responsibility caught hold among both Republican and Democratic politicians, so much so that it found its way into the title of the 1996 welfare reform bill: the Personal Responsibility and Work Opportunity Reconciliation Act (PRWORA).

PRWORA changed a major part of the American safety net profoundly. It ended AFDC and replaced it with Temporary Assistance for Needy Families (TANF), which placed a lifetime limit of five years on the benefits anyone could receive—though it allowed individual states to have even lower lifetime limits. Payments to states became block grants that states could largely distribute and use how they wanted; some states put

45

Documented immigrants can access social safety net programs, though laws control how and when they may receive assistance. Uncodumented immigrants can't.

most of the money toward scholarships, while others used it for more traditional welfare payments.

PRWORA also dramatically increased work requirements for welfare recipients and made work programs a condition of states receiving block grants. Additionally, it limited how long someone could be unemployed and receiving welfare payments. Unwed mothers who were under eighteen had their access to TANF limited; the requirements of TANF were crafted specifically to encourage two-parent families.[3]

PRWORA had a profound effect on the social safety net. It removed people from welfare—not necessarily by raising them out of poverty, but by kicking them off TANF after their five years had expired, leaving them to fend for themselves. In Minnesota, for example, 89 percent of poor families received AFDC in 1995; in 2014, only 41 percent of poor families were receiving assistance. The percentage of poor families receiving TANF has decreased since PRWORA was signed, but the number of families living in extreme poverty has increased.[4]

Children's Health Insurance Program

One of Bill Clinton's other major campaign promises was to bring about comprehensive health-care reform, with an aim to providing universal health care to all Americans. His efforts and those of First Lady Hillary Clinton were ultimately unsuccessful in the face of an onslaught of negative advertising funded by the health insurance and pharmaceutical industries as well as various conservative groups.

With universal health care out of reach, proponents of reform targeted uninsured children. Senators Ted Kennedy and Orrin Hatch sponsored a bill that drew bipartisan support: the Children's Health Insurance Program (CHIP). It acts under Title XXI of the SSA and is effectively an extension of Medicaid. As such, while the federal government sets certain requirements, states administer CHIP for themselves. It targets

Immigrants and Welfare

Contrary to popular belief, undocumented immigrants have never been able to access federal welfare programs. Only documented immigrants, including refugees and asylum seekers, can do this. PRWORA limits federal benefits—including Medicaid, SNAP, CHIP, TANF, and SSI—to documented immigrants who have been in the United States for at least five years.

When the law was passed, many documented immigrants were immediately kicked off federal programs because they had not been in residence long enough. However, states could still choose to use their own funding to give immigrants aid. As of 2019, twenty-six states have done so.[5]

In recent years, CHIP has come under attack in the Senate, despite having expanded coverage and care for some of the most vulnerable members of society.

children whose families make too much money to qualify for Medicaid but not enough to afford private health insurance, up to 200 percent of the federal poverty level.[6]

A 2014 Kaiser Family Foundation study found that CHIP has been successful in expanding coverage to uninsured children and has helped reduce health-care disparities that greatly affect vulnerable populations. Between 1997 and 2014, the uninsured rate went from 14 percent to 7 percent.[7] CHIP has been reauthorized every time the bill has come up, though not always without conflict and debate. The program has been extended through 2027.[8]

The Health-Care Safety Net Expands

In 2001, researchers at Harvard Medical School conducted a study of five states that found that "medical problems contributed to at least 46.2 percent of all bankruptcies." After receiving considerable pushback and debates over the data, the study was revisited in 2007. The results were even more startling: "Using a conservative definition, 62.1 percent of all bankruptcies in 2007 were medical ... Most medical debtors were well-educated, owned homes, and had middle-class occupations. Three quarters had health insurance." Worse, comparing the 2001 and 2007 study showed that medical bankruptcies had increased by nearly 50 percent in just six years.[1]

Health care and medical debt were growing problems that the social safety net of the early 2000s wasn't made to catch. Medicaid and other programs covered the poorest, but it was people who didn't seem like they should need the safety net who found themselves in trouble. Throughout the 2000s and into the 2010s, that part of the safety net received the most attention, though there was also expansion in other areas.

Medical debt is a growing problem; from 2001 to 2007, medical bankruptcies increased by 50 percent, even for people who had private health insurance.

The Medicare Modernization Act

President George W. Bush signed the Medicare Modernization Act (MMA) in 2003. The law was considered a major overhaul of the Medicare system. MMA required higher fees to be paid by wealthier Medicare users and gave extra funding to rural hospitals.

MMA created health savings accounts (HSAs), which could be used by people who were still working. An HSA allows someone to take a percentage of their pretax income and place it in a savings account that can only be used for medical expenses their health insurance plan won't cover.

The biggest effect of MMA was that it created Medicare Part D, which was a voluntary Medicare plan that covered prescription drugs.[2] Medicare Part D was criticized for not allowing the government to negotiate prices with drug companies, which in other countries allows drug prices to be significantly lower. In fact, MMA allowed only insurance companies to negotiate drug prices and introduced a large coverage gap that became known as the "donut hole."[3]

Supplemental Nutrition Assistance Program (SNAP)

In the 1990s, some states had already begun phasing out actual food stamps and replacing them with special debit cards under a program called Electronic Benefit Transfer (EBT). The 2008 Farm Bill made EBT standard across the United States and renamed the food stamp program SNAP (short for Supplemental Nutrition Assistance Program) to fight the social stigma against food stamps.

Food-stamp programs had long focused on nutrition education and improved access to food stamps, but the 2008 Farm Bill specifically included those goals as the mission of SNAP. Benefits were also increased for most households. Bush attempted to veto the Farm Bill but was overridden by Congress.[4]

Housing First

Prior to 2005, housing for the homeless was modeled on people being "housing ready." For homeless people to receive government housing, they had to prove themselves ready by undergoing counseling and addiction treatment.

Despite his well-earned reputation as a conservative, President George W. Bush directed HUD to institute what can be seen as a radically liberal policy for federal housing programs: housing first. Homeless people were given free housing without strings attached. Counselors and social workers were made available to new residents, but it was up to the formerly homeless people to choose to utilize these resources, rather than having the resources forced on them as a requirement for housing.

Many homeless families receive assistance from shelters and missions, and as economic troubles deepen in communities, the strain on such facilities rises.

The housing-first concept showed immediate success. There was a 30 percent decline in the chronically homeless population between 2005 and 2007. Of the chronically homeless who were given housing, 80 percent stayed off the streets for at least two years. Many cities in the United States have begun to follow HUD's example.[5]

Housing-first policies continued under President Barack Obama in his Opening Doors program, which saw another 27 percent drop in chronic homelessness between 2010 and 2016.[6] The fate of federal housing-first policies has become uncertain since the election of 2016; for all their success, these programs have often proven unpopular with conservatives.

The American Recovery and Reinvestment Act of 2009

When the housing bubble burst in late 2007, the United States experienced the Great Recession of 2008, which caused financial problems for the majority of the population. Newly elected president Barack Obama made emergency financial aid and recovery from the Great Recession his major priority, calling for an economic stimulus similar to what was undertaken during the Great Depression.

The American Recovery and Reinvestment Act focused on preserving and creating new jobs and giving aid to those who had been hit hard by the recession, from individuals to state and local governments. It accomplished this through a combination of tax incentives for individuals and companies, monetary aid for health care, education aid such as extra Pell Grant funding,

What Is an Entitlement?

The word "entitlement" has a negative connotation, perhaps because it's often used to mean "a belief that one inherently deserves special treatment." Public programs in the United States such as Social Security and Medicare have been defended as an earned benefit, not an entitlement, because people pay into them with their taxes. There is a common and erroneous view that an entitlement is negative and unearned, with politicians often eager to make the meaning even more confusing.

However, an entitlement from the government means a program that people automatically get the benefits from if they're eligible. It's not a negative thing. Social Security is an entitlement. If you're a US citizen, you're entitled to receive Social Security benefits.

extra funding for SNAP, extra weeks of unemployment benefits, and infrastructure investment programs to directly create jobs.[7]

In 2010, 82 percent of economic experts polled by IGM Forum agreed or strongly agreed that unemployment was lower at the end of 2010 than it would have been without the act. Furthermore, 56 percent of the experts agreed that the benefits outweighed the costs.[8]

The Affordable Care Act

During his campaign for office, President Obama said, "We have to fix our health-care system, which is putting an enormous burden on families … They are getting crushed, and many of them are going bankrupt as a consequence of health care."[9] After his election, he continued to make health-care reform a top priority. After much debate in Congress and despite escalating protests by the new Tea Party movement, which supported less government involvement in citizens' lives, the Patient Protection and Affordable Care Act—often shortened to ACA—was signed into law by Obama on March 23, 2010.[10]

The ACA was a massive law with many provisions that aimed to strengthen access to health care, making it a major part of the current American social safety net. The ACA placed new regulations on insurance companies; for example, it specified what essential health services had to be covered and no longer allowed insurance companies to deny coverage due to preexisting conditions or drop people when they became sick and expensive. Government-run insurance exchanges were mandated, with subsidies for low-income people to help them buy private health insurance.[11]

Medicaid expanded under the ACA, but the Supreme Court ruled that the expansion had to be voluntary for the states. As a result, many Republican-controlled states refused to expand Medicaid; some were later forced to do so by voter initiatives.

In 2010, President Barack Obama (*center*) signed the Affordable Care Act into law. The historic bill was passed without a single Republican vote in favor of it.

In 2018, Idaho and Utah citizens voted to expand Medicaid, though the state governments have since attempted to get around these initiatives.[12]

After Republicans took control of the House in 2011, they voted more than fifty times to repeal the ACA or otherwise stop it from working.[13] However, even with Republicans in total control of the government starting in 2017, they were unable to agree on a way of repealing the ACA and replacing it before the midterm elections of 2018 caused them to lose the House.[14]

The future of American health care will likely be determined by the policies of presidents and representatives yet to come.

What Does the Future Hold?

In March 2018, the Congressional Budget Office (CBO) conducted a study about household income. Using data from 2014 (the most recent and complete data set it had), the CBO found that income inequality in the United States had increased significantly since 1979. Its report stated that this increase "largely stems from the significant increase in inequality of market income ... which has been driven primarily by substantial income growth at the top of the distribution." In other words, the rich are getting richer, but the poor are staying poor. This growing inequality is only partially offset by social safety net programs—and the safety net as it exists isn't a long-term solution.[1] What does the future hold for America?

Privatization

When George W. Bush signed MMA, one provision in the law was to run a pilot study in several cities to partially privatize Medicare. After his reelection in 2005, President Bush also pushed to privatize Social Security; his attempt to do so was unsuccessful after loud protests led by senior citizen advocate groups. President Bush's plan would have had Social Security

Continued efforts to privatize Social Security have been met with refusals and protests. Critics argue that private companies often focus on profit ahead of care.

become a private savings account dependent on the stock market—which could mean big losses or big gains for retirees, dependent upon Wall Street.[2] In 2016, Speaker of the House Paul Ryan put forward another plan to privatize Medicare, which was also unsuccessful.[3]

The question of privatization is complex and often split along ideological and political lines; it's highly dependent upon whether someone believes that private enterprise and the free market are always beneficial to consumers. Privatization may lower government costs in the short run or long run, but private companies may have different goals than the government when providing a service. For example, it is in the interest of a private company such as a health insurer to discourage the most expensive people from utilizing its services because private companies first maximize profit.[4] The debate about privatization of government functions is ongoing.

Universal Health Care

While the ACA helped many more people attain health insurance, it hasn't achieved universal coverage of all

Universal Health Care Around the World

A major reason why universal health care is such a hot topic in America is that out of thirty-three developed countries in the world, the United States is the only one without some kind of universal health care system. The other thirty-two countries use one of three models:

Single-Payer: Citizens pay taxes, and the government spends this money to provide health care anyone can access. Canada and the United Kingdom have this.

Insurance Mandate: Everyone is required to buy health insurance, generally either from a private, nonprofit company or from the government. The Netherlands uses this model.

Combination: The government pays for some levels of health care, but citizens can choose to pay for other levels of care. Australia and Singapore have this system.[5]

No one knows what the future will bring for American health care, but vocal citizens continue to make it clear that everyone, no matter their background or income, deserves good care.

Americans. According to the Census Bureau, 28 million people were uninsured as of 2017, and those who use private insurance still face many of the old problems of high deductibles and confusing rules about which doctors they can see. This has brought the idea of universal health care back into broad public debate.

There are several potential plans for bringing about universal health care in the United States. One popular idea is to move to a single-payer system, in which the government would be the single provider of health insurance. This might involve expanding Medicare to cover all Americans or giving Americans the option to buy into Medicare for a small percentage of their annual income. There are debates on whether private health insurance should be phased out, if it may be competed out of existence, or if private health insurance would persist as extra insurance people might buy in addition to Medicare.[6]

Free College, Universal Pre-K

Education has long been viewed as the sure path to a well-paying job and a good standard of living, which is why loans and grants are part of our safety net programs. However, grants and scholarships have fallen behind the rising cost of college tuition, meaning that students have taken on more debt. Meanwhile, many students have found that the jobs that are available after they graduate no longer offer high enough salaries to pay down that debt. As of 2018, more than 44 million people had student loan debt, totaling $1.5 trillion. The average student who graduated with a bachelor's degree in 2016 owed $37,172 in student loans.[7]

In his 2015 State of the Union Address, President Obama said he wanted everyone to have access to two years of free community college. Other Democratic politicians—such as Bernie Sanders, Cory Booker, Elizabeth Warren, Julián Castro, and Kamala Harris—have embraced the idea of free or debt-free four-year college. Some plans involve free tuition only, while others include the additional costs of books, housing, and food during college, with the goal of allowing students to graduate without debt.[8]

Additionally, some Democratic politicians, such as Kamala Harris, argue for universal pre-K. Currently, preschool for four- and five-year-olds is generally only available through fees paid to schools. Universal pre-K would allow children to have full-day preschool for free. Proponents argue this would help

The rising cost of a college education has caused many young Americans to live with debt. Protests are sometimes held for young adults to voice their strong feelings about the price of college and the failures of this part of the social safety net.

vulnerable populations close early education gaps and allow parents to return to work sooner or avoid the cost of daycare.[9]

Universal Basic Income

One of the most radical proposals for the safety net is what's called universal basic income (UBI). The idea behind UBI is that if every person were provided with a stipend from the government (which they could spend however they like), poverty would be effectively eliminated. This stipend would be enough to provide a decent standard of living and could be supplemented by wages from a job if the person chose to work.

UBI is not necessarily a new idea, even if it has become a topic of conversation in the tech sector as billionaire CEOs have begun to worry about automation-caused unemployment.[10] The oldest trial of UBI was run in Manitoba, Canada from 1974 to 1978 and was called Mincome. During the trial, the people in the program showed improved mental health, underwent fewer hospitalizations, and completed more schooling. The employment rate didn't change in the town, despite fears that it would cause people to leave their jobs.[11] Other pilot programs have been run more recently in several other countries, including Finland and Kenya.[12]

There are many other ways the social safety net could change in the future—more than could be talked about in a book ten times as long as this one. There might be a Green New Deal that guarantees jobs in new industries and combats climate change. There could be expanded housing-first programs until no one is homeless anymore. The social safety net might be eliminated entirely, cut in favor of lower taxes.

What future would you imagine for America?

1893 An economic depression starts in the United States and lasts for four years.

1894 Coxey's Army marches on Washington, DC, reaching its destination on April 30. Coxey is put in a workhouse for walking on the Capitol lawn.

1911 Wisconsin passes the first comprehensive workers' compensation law in America.

1914 World War I begins, though the United States does not enter the war until 1917. It ends on November 11, 1918.

1929 The Great Depression begins with the stock market crash on October 29.

1932 The Great Depression deepens, and 25 percent of Americans are unemployed.

1933 The Civil Works Administration begins to provide temporary employment with public works projects. Congress disbands it in 1934.

1935 The Social Security Act is passed, in part guaranteeing unemployment insurance for workers who have lost their jobs and providing for the elderly and disabled.

1939 World War II begins, though the United States does not formally enter the war until after the attack on Pearl Harbor on December 7, 1941.

1945 World War II ends.

1963 President John F. Kennedy is assassinated on November 22. Shortly thereafter, Vice President Lyndon B. Johnson becomes president.

1964 President Johnson declares a "War on Poverty" in his first State of the Union address. Food stamps become a permanent national program.

1965 President Johnson signs the Elementary and Secondary Education Act. Medicare and Medicaid become law under the Social Security Act, with Medicare forcing the desegregation of hospitals by the end of 1966.

1968 Dr. Martin Luther King Jr. is assassinated. The backlash against racial gains due to safety net and antipoverty programs begins in earnest with the election of Richard Nixon.

1972 Supplemental Security Income becomes law and begins to provide supplemental income for elderly and disabled people. The WIC program begins as well.

1974 The Section 8 housing program begins.

1976 Ronald Reagan campaigns unsuccessfully for president with stories about the "welfare queen."

1978 The earned income tax credit becomes permanent, as a way to provide financial aid to the working poor.

1982 Under President Reagan, the largest tax cuts in history cause major spending reductions to antipoverty and social safety net programs.

1996 President Bill Clinton signs the Personal Responsibility and Work Opportunity Reconciliation Act, signaling the "end [of] welfare as we have come to know it." Welfare as it was created in the Social Security Act becomes Temporary Assistance for Needy Families, with a five-year benefit limit.

1997 The Children's Health Insurance Program (CHIP) begins to cover children in poor families.

2005 President Bush directs HUD to pursue housing-first programs for the homeless.

2007 The housing bubble bursts, throwing America into the Great Recession, which continues through 2008 and into 2009.

2008 Food stamps become the Supplemental Nutrition Assistance Program (SNAP) after Congress overrides President George W. Bush's veto on the Farm Bill.

2009 President Barack Obama signs the American Recovery and Reinvestment Act of 2009 in an effort to bring the Great Recession to an end before it could become a depression.

2010 President Obama signs the Patient Protection and Affordable Care Act, expanding private health insurance coverage via government subsidies.

2014 The Congressional Budget Office publishes a report that shows income inequality has increased significantly since 1979, "primarily driven by substantial income growth at the top of the [income] distribution."

2018 The federal government shuts down on December 22 due to funding disagreements about a border wall between the United States and Mexico; 800,000 federal workers suddenly find themselves dependent on the social safety net.

2019 The Trump administration seeks to redefine poverty by replacing the Consumer Price Index, which is used to estimate the federal poverty line.

CHAPTER NOTES

Introduction

1. "Donald Trump's Border Wall Is Unpopular with a Majority of American Voters, New Gallup Poll Finds," *Salon*, February 4, 2019, www.salon.com/2019/02/04/donald-trumps-border-wall-is-unpopular-with-a-majority-of-american-voters-new-gallup-poll-finds.

2. "Trump's Shutdown Is Forcing Over 400,000 Federal Employees to Work Without Pay," *In These Times*, January 18, 2019, inthesetimes.com/working/entry/21691/trump_shutdown_federal_workers_lockout_strike.

3. "Government Shutdown Threatens to Have Bigger Impact on Economy," CNBC, January 10, 2019, www.cnbc.com/2019/01/10/government-shutdown-could-start-to-hit-economy-as-it-moves-into-uncharted-territory.html.

4. "States Report Sharp Increase in Unemployment Claims by Federal Workers as Shutdown Approaches One Month," *Washington Post,* January 17, 2019, www.washingtonpost.com/national/states-report-sharp-increase-in-unemployment-claims-by-federal-workers/2019/01/17/e1f6b566-19f7-11e9-8813-cb9dec761e73_story.html.

5. "Federal Employees Turn to Food Banks to Feed Their Families During Shutdown," CNN, January 20, 2019, www.cnn.com/2019/01/17/us/government-employees-shutdown-food-banks/index.html.

6. "NYS Agencies to Offer Help to Furloughed Federal Workers," WKBW Buffalo, January 17, 2019, www.wkbw.com/news/local-news/nys-agencies-to-offer-help-to-furloughed-federal-workers.

7. "NYS Agencies to Offer Help to Furloughed Federal Workers," WKBW Buffalo.

8. "Low-Wage Workers: Poverty and the Use of Selected Federal Social Safety Net Programs Persist Among Working Families," Government Accountability Office, GAO-17-677, September 22, 2017.

CHAPTER 1: Without a Net

1. "Poorhouses Were Designed to Punish People for Their Poverty," History.com, www.history.com/news/in-the-19th-century-the-last-place-you-wanted-to-go-was-the-poorhouse. "Poor Relief and the Almshouse," VCU Libraries Social Welfare History Project, socialwelfare.library.vcu.edu/issues/poor-relief-almshouse.

2. "Understanding Mutual Benefit Societies at the Turn of the Twentieth Century," *Division II Faculty Publications*, Paper 77, 2001.

3. "How a Ragtag Band of Reformers Organized the First Protest March on Washington, D.C.," *Smithsonian*, May 1, 2014, www.smithsonianmag.com/smithsonian-institution/how-ragtag-band-reformers-organized-first-protest-march-washington-dc-180951270.

4. "Laura Ingalls Wilder and One of the Greatest Natural Disasters in American History," lithub.com, December 5, 2017, lithub.com/laura-ingalls-wilder-and-the-greatest-natural-disaster-in-american-history. "Grasshopper Plagues, 1873–1877," MNopedia.org, last updated April 17, 2018, www.mnopedia.org/event/grasshopper-plagues-1873-1877.

5. "A Brief History of Workers' Compensation," *Iowa Orthopaedic Journal*, v. 19, 1999.

CHAPTER 2: The Great Depression

1. "The Great Depression," PBS, accessed on February 27, 2019, www.pbs.org/wgbh/americanexperience/features/dustbowl-great-depression.

2. "Hoovervilles and Homelessness," Great Depression in Washington State, accessed on February 27, 2019, depts.washington.edu/depress/hooverville.shtml.

3. "Family Experiences and New Deal Relief," National Archives, last updated December 20, 2017, www.archives.gov/publications/prologue/2012/fall/fera.html. "Works Progress Administration (WPA)," History.com, July 13, 2017, www.history.com/topics/great-depression/works-progress-administration.

4. "The Social Security Act of 1935," SSA.gov, accessed on February 27, 2019, www.ssa.gov/history/35act.html.

5. Wolfgang M Rudorf, "The Housing Division of the Public Works Administration in Its Architectural Context," Massachusetts Institute of Technology Thesis, 1984, hdl.handle.net/1721.1/42966. "The Federal Housing Administration (FHA)," HUD.gov, accessed on February 27, 2019, www.hud.gov/program_offices/housing/fhahistory.

6. "The Racial Segregation of American Cities Was Anything but Accidental," Smithsonian, May 30, 2017, www.smithsonianmag.com/history/how-federal-government-intentionally-racially-segregated-american-cities-180963494.

7. "Modern-Day Redlining: How Banks Block People of Color from Homeownership," Chicago Tribune, February 17, 2018, www.chicagotribune.com/business/ct-biz-modern-day-redlining-20180215-story.html.

8. "A 'Forgotten History' of How the U.S. Government Segregated America," NPR, May 3, 2017, www.npr.org/2017/05/03/5266 55831/a-forgotten-history-of-how-the-u-s-government-segregated -america.

CHAPTER 3: The Great Society

1. John F. Kennedy, "Democratic National Convention Nomination Acceptance Address," July 15, 1960, video via AmericanRhetoric .com, www.americanrhetoric.com/speeches/jfk1960dnc.htm.

2. "Chapter 6: Eras of the New Frontier and the Great Society 1961–1969," US Department of Labor, accessed on February 27, 2019, www.dol.gov/general/about dol/history/dolchp06.

3. "The Great Society," PBS, accessed on February 27, 2019, www.pbs. org/johngardner/chapters/4c.html.

4. "America's Longest War," CNN, January 8, 2014, www .cnn.com/2014/01/08/politics/war-on-poverty-50-years/index.html.

5. "America's Longest War," CNN.

6. Committee on Examination of the Adequacy of Food Resources and SNAP Allotments, et al., *Supplemental Nutrition Assistance Program: Examining the Evidence to Define Benefit Adequacy* (Washington, DC: National Academies Press, 2013). History, Background, and Goals of the Supplemental Nutrition Assistance Program, www.ncbi.nlm.nih.gov/books/NBK206907.

7. "Evaluating the Success of the Great Society," *Washington Post*, May 17, 2014, www.washingtonpost.com/wp-srv/special/national/ great-society-at-50.

8. "Elementary and Secondary Education Act of 1965," VCU Libraries Social Welfare History Project, accessed on February 27, 2019, socialwelfare.library.vcu.edu/programs/education/elementary-and-secondary-education-act-of-1965.

9. "Did the Black Panthers Create the WIC Food Program?," Snopes, February 6, 2018, www.snopes.com/fact-check/black-panthers-wic-food-program.

10. "History of SSA During the Johnson Administration 1963–1968," SSA.gov, accessed on February 27, 2019, www.ssa.gov/history/ssa/lbjmedicare1.html.

11. Bruce C. Vladeck, Paul N. Van de Water, and June Eichner (eds), *Strengthening Medicare's Role in Reducing Racial and Ethnic Health Disparities*, National Academy of Social Insurance, October 2006.

Chapter 4: Reforms Begin

1. "The Great Society and the Drive for Black Equality," Digital History, accessed on February 27, 2019, www.digitalhistory.uh.edu/disp_textbook.cfm?smtID=2&psid=3333.

2. "White Backlash," Digital History, accessed on February 27, 2019, www.digitalhistory.uh.edu/disp_textbook.cfm?smtid=2&psid=3334.

3. "Benign Neglect: The Realpolitik of Race and Ethnicity," in *An American Quarter Century: US Politics from Vietnam to Clinton* (Manchester, UK: Manchester University Press, 1995).

4. "Supplemental Security Income," VCU Libraries Social Welfare History Project, accessed on February 27, 2019, socialwelfare.library.vcu.edu/public-welfare/public-welfare-supplemental-security-income.

5. "Meals on Wheels America: The Issues," Meals on Wheels America, accessed on February 27, 2019, www.mealsonwheelsamerica.org/ learn-more/the-issue.

6. "WIC Program Overview and History," National WIC Association, accessed on February 27, 2019, www.nwica.org/overview-and-history.

7. Jimmy Carter, "Education Amendments of 1978 and the Middle Income Student Assistance Act Statement on Signing H. R. 15 and S. 2539 into Law," November 1, 1978.

8. "Section 8 Program Background Information," HUD.gov, accessed on February 27, 2019, www.hud.gov/program_offices/housing/mfh/ rfp/s8bkinfo.

9. "How Section 8 Became a 'Racial Slur,'" *Washington Post*, June 15, 2015, www.washingtonpost.com/news/wonk/wp/2015/06/15/how-section-8-became-a-racial-slur.

10. Margot L. Crandall-Hollick, "The Earned Income Tax Credit: EITC: A Brief Legislative History," Congressional Research Service Report, March 20, 2018.

CHAPTER 5: The "Welfare Queen"

1. "The Welfare Queen," *Slate*, December 2013, www.slate.com/ articles/news_and_politics/history/2013/12/linda_taylor_welfare_ queen_ronald_reagan_made_her_a_notorious_american_villain .html.

2. "Reforming the Welfare System: The Family Support Act of 1988; Symposium on Poverty," *Journal of Legislation*, vol. 16, issue 2, article 2, 1990.

3. "Welfare Offers Short-Term Help and Long-Term Poverty, Thanks to Asset Tests," *Forbes*, October 13, 2016, www.forbes.com/ sites/jeffreydorfman/2016/10/13/welfare-offers-short-term-help -and-long-term-poverty.

4. Committee on Examination of the Adequacy of Food Resources and SNAP Allotments, et al., *Supplemental Nutrition Assistance Program: Examining the Evidence to Define Benefit Adequacy*.

5. "Social Welfare Under Reagan," CQ Researcher, accessed on February 27, 2019, library.cqpress.com/cqresearcher/document. php?id=cqresrre1984030900.

CHAPTER 6: The End of Welfare as We Know It

1. "Why Bill Clinton Signed the Welfare Reform Bill, as Explained in 1996," *Time*, August 19, 2016, time.com/4446348/welfare -reform-20-years.

2. "How the Rhetoric of Responsibility Hurts the Welfare State," *New Republic*, June 22, 2017, newrepublic.com/article/143462/rhetoric-responsibility-hurts-welfare-state.

3. "Welfare and the Minimum Wage: Are Workfare Participants 'Employees' Under the Fair Labor Standards Act?," *University of Chicago Law Review*, vol. 66, no. 1, Winter 1999.

4. "The End of Welfare as We Know It," *Atlantic*, April 1, 2016, www. theatlantic.com/business/archive/2016/04/the-end-of-welfare -as-we-know-it/476322.

5. "Fact Sheet: Immigrants and Public Benefits," National Immigration Forum, August 21, 2018, immigrationforum.org/article/fact-sheet-immigrants-and-public-benefits.

6. "Program History," Medicaid.gov, accessed on February 27, 2019, www.medicaid.gov/about-us/program-history/index.html.

7. "The Impact of the Children's Health Insurance Program (CHIP): What Does the Research Tell Us?," Kaiser Commission on Medicaid and the Uninsured, July 2014 Issue Brief, kaiserfamilyfoundation.files.wordpress.com/2014/07/8615 -the-impact-of-the-children_s-health-insurance-program-chip -what-does-the-research-tell-us.pdf.

8. 111 Stat. 251

CHAPTER 7: The Heath-Care Safety Net Expands

1. "Medical Bankruptcy in the United States, 2007: Results of a National Study," *American Journal of Medicine*, vol. 122, no. 8, August 2009.

2. Public Law 108–173.

3. "Searching for Savings in Medicare Drug Price Negotiations," KFF. org, April 26, 2018, www.kff.org/medicare/issue-brief/searching-for-savings-in-medicare-drug-price-negotiations.

4. "A Short History of SNAP," USDA, accessed on February 27, 2019, www.fns.usda.gov/snap/short-history-snap.

5. "Bush Administration Has Housed Many Homeless," McClatchy DC Bureau, October 26, 2008, www.mcclatchydc.com/news/politics-government/article24505888.html.

6. "Nationwide, Homelessness Plunged Under Obama," CityLab .com, November 18, 2016, www.citylab.com/equity/2016/11/homelessness-obama-trump/508223/.

7. 123 Stat. 115.

8. "Economic Stimulus (revisited)," IGM Forum, July 29, 2014, www. igmchicago.org/surveys/economic-stimulus-revisited.

9. "The First Presidential Debate (Transcript)," *New York Times*, September 26, 2008, www.nytimes.com/elections/2008/president/debates/transcripts/first-presidential-debate.html.

10. Daniel Skinner, "'Keep Your Government Hands Off My Medicare!': An Analysis of Media Effects on Tea Party Health Care Politics," *New Political Science*, 34, December 2012.

11. 124 Stat. 119 through 124 Stat. 1025

12. "Idaho and Utah Lawmakers Target Medicaid Expansion and 'Will of the People,'" 91.5 KRCC, February 25, 2019, www.krcc.org/post/idaho-and-utah-lawmakers-target-medicaid-expansion-and-will-people.

13. "Reminder: The House Voted to Repeal Obamacare More Than 50 Times," *Time*, March 24, 2017, time.com/4712725/ahca-house-repeal-votes-obamacare.

14. "Republicans Abandon the Fight to Repeal and Replace Obama's Healthcare Law," *Washington Post*, November 7, 2018, www.washingtonpost.com/powerpost/republicans-abandon-the-fight-to-repeal-and-replace-obamas-health-care-law/2018/11/07/157d052c-e2d8-11e8-ab2c-b31dcd53ca6b_story.html.

CHAPTER 8: What Does the Future Hold?

1. "The Distribution of Household Income, 2014," Congress of the United States Congressional Budget Office, March 2018, www.cbo.gov/system/files/115th-congress-2017-2018/reports/53597-distribution-household-income-2014.pdf.

2. "Privatization Is Really a Plan to Dismantle Social Security," CNBC, March 26, 2018, www.cnbc.com/2018/03/26/privatization-is-really-a-plan-to-dismantle-social-security.html.

3. "Paul Ryan's Plan to Change Medicare Looks a Lot Like Obamacare," NPR, November 26, 2016, www.npr.org/sections/health-shots/2016/11/26/503158039/paul-ryans-plan-to-change-medicare-looks-a-lot-like-obamacare.

4. "The Privatization of the Health and Human Services: Parsing the Roles of the Public and Private Sectors," *People, Politics, and Policy*, issue 3: February 2012.

5. "Universal Health Care in Different Countries, Pros and Cons of Each," thebalance.com, December 24, 2018, www.thebalance.com/universal-health-care-4156211.

6. "Universal Healthcare Was Unthinkable in America, but Not Any More," *Guardian*, September 16, 2018, www.theguardian .com/commentisfree/2018/sep/16/medicare-for-all-universal -healthcare-democrats.

7. "Student Loan Debt Statistics in 2018: A $1.5 Trillion Crisis," *Forbes*, June 13, 2018, www.forbes.com/sites/zackfriedman/ 2018/06/13/student-loan-debt-statistics-2018.

8. "The College-Affordability Crisis Is Uniting Democratic Candidates," *Atlantic*, February 26, 2019, www.theatlantic.com/ education/archive/2019/02/2020-democrats-free-college/583585.

9. "'Day Care for All': How America Views Universal Pre-K," WBUR, February 19, 2019, www.wbur.org/onpoint/2019/02/19/day -care-for-all-universal-pre-k-child-care-working-families.

10. "Elon Musk: Free Cash Handouts 'Will Be Necessary' if Robots Take Humans' Jobs," CNBC, June 18, 2018, www.cnbc.com/ 2018/06/18/elon-musk-automated-jobs-could-make-ubi-cash -handouts-necessary.html.

11. "Money for Nothing: The Truth About Universal Basic Income," *Nature*, May 30, 2018, www.nature.com/articles/d41586-018 -05259-x.

12. "Universal Basic Income Had a Rough 2018," *MIT Technology Review*, December 27, 2018, www.technologyreview.com/s/612 640/universal-basic-income-had-a-rough-2018.

GLOSSARY

conservation Preservation and protection of wild lands and wildlife, sometimes in a way that still makes it accessible for public enjoyment.

entitlement A government program that provides benefits to anyone who meets its requirements.

grant Money that does not need to be paid back that is given to someone by a government or organization.

Hoovervilles Massive homeless camps during the Great Depression, named thus because homelessness was blamed on President Hoover.

loan Money that is given to someone that must be paid back, normally with interest so that the sum paid back will be larger than the original sum given.

means tested Welfare that is given only to people who have below a certain income or amount of wealth.

moral panic Concern and fear spreading through society over the perception of some evil that threatens the well-being of good citizens or the society itself.

pilot program A small-scale, short-term experimental program that provides information on how the program might run on a large scale and in the long term.

poorhouse An institution where poor people were sent before a social safety net was in place.

privatize To transfer an industry, program, or service from public ownership and administration to private control, often for profit.

redlining The systematic denial of services (such as mortgage insurance) to racial communities.

segregation The enforced separation of racial groups in communities and establishments.

social safety net Welfare programs that protect people from poverty and hardship.

standard of living The wealth and material comfort available to a person or community.

stigma Disgrace associated with particular circumstances, groups, or qualities.

BOOKS

Desmond, Matthew. *Evicted: Poverty and Profit in the American City*. New York, NY: Broadway Books, 2017.

Edin, Kathryn, and Luke H. Shaefer. *$2.00 a Day: Living on Almost Nothing in America*. Wilmington, MA: Mariner Books, 2016.

Rothstein, Richard. *The Color of Law: A Forgotten History of How Our Government Segregated America*. New York, NY: Liveright, 2017.

WEBSITES

The Great Depression in Washington State
depts.washington.edu/depress/index.shtml
Detailed articles reveal how the Great Depression affected life in Washington State.

The Living Wage Calculator
livingwage.mit.edu
This interactive website features articles about the living wage and a calculator that shows what that might be in various American counties.

SPENT
playspent.org
This simulator run by Urban Ministries of Durham educates users on the choices required by poverty and homelessness.

VCU Libraries Social Welfare History Project
socialwelfare.library.vcu.edu
Articles on this website cover historical topics on the social safety net.

INDEX